W9-ASR-761

DATE DUE

Super Senses

Special Animal Senses

Mary Mackill

Heinemann Library
Chicago, Illinois

© 2006 Heinemann Library
a division of Reed Elsevier Inc.
Chicago, Illinois

Customer Service 888-454-2279

Visit our website at www.heinemannraintree.com

Printed and bound in China by South China Printing Company Limited
Photo research by Hannah Taylor and Fiona Orbell
Designed by Jo Hinton-Malivoire and bigtop

10 09 08 07 06
10 9 8 7 6 5 4 3 2 1

Library of Congress Cataloging-in-Publication Data
Mackill, Mary.
   Special animal senses / Mary Mackill.
      p. cm. -- (Super senses.)
   Includes bibliographical references and index.
   ISBN 1-4034-7378-1 (library binding-hardcover : alk. paper) -- ISBN 1-4034-7385-4 (pbk. : alk. paper)
 1. Senses and sensation--Juvenile literature. 2. Animal behavior--Juvenile literature. I. Title. II.
Series: Mackill, Mary. Super senses.
QP434.M34 2006
612.8--dc22

                              2005018940

Acknowledgments
The publishers would like to thank the following for permission to reproduce photographs:
Alamy Images pp. **5** (eWILDz), **9** (Imagestate), **13** (Kevin Schafer), **17**, **23a** (Robert Harding Picture Library); Corbis pp. **7**, **10**, **22tl**, **24l** (royalty free), **12**, **22tr**, **24r** (Gallo Images; Nigel J. Dennis), **4**, **23c** (Norbert Schafer), **6** (Tom Stewart); Getty Images pp. **20** (Digital Vision), **14** (Photodisc), **11**, **15**, **22bl**, **24cl** (The Image Bank); naturepl.com pp. **18**, **23b** (John Downer), **21** (Michael Pitts), **8** (Peter Reese); Photolibrary.com pp. **16**, **23d**; Science Photo Library pp. **19**, **22br**, **24cr** (Georgette Douwma).

Cover photograph reproduced with permission of Alamy Images/Martin Harvey.

Every effort has been made to contact copyright holders of any material reproduced in this book. Any omissions will be rectified in subsequent printings if notice is given to
the publisher.

Many thanks to the teachers, library media specialists, reading instructors, and educational consultants who have helped develop the Read and Learn/Lee y aprende brand.

Contents

Some words are shown in bold, **like this**. You can find out what they mean by looking in the glossary.

What Are Senses?

Humans can see, hear, smell, touch, and taste.

These are your **senses**.

Did you know most animals have the same senses as you?

Why Are Senses Important?

Your **senses** tell you about the world around you.

Animals live in many different places.

Their senses tell them what is around them, too.

Super Spotters

Some animals have a super **sense** of sight!

Owls are good at seeing in the dark.

A chameleon can look at two
different things at the same time!

Super Listeners

Some animals are good at hearing.

Elephants can hear sounds that are too low for us to hear.

Some animals, such as foxes, have large ears that they can move.

They listen for sounds all around them.

Super Sniffers

Animals that cannot see well often have a good **sense** of smell.

An aardvark uses its special nose to smell for food.

Ants follow a smell to find their way home.

Super Tasters

Some animals have a super **sense** of taste.

An earthworm has taste buds all over its body!

Did you know a butterfly can taste with its feet?

Super Feelers

whisker

Animals use touch to tell them where they are.

A catfish has lots of **whiskers** to touch things around it.

antennae

A snail uses its **antennae** to touch.

If it does not know what something is, it will go back into its shell.

Super Travelers

Pigeons have a **sense** called **homing**.

A special part of their brain tells them which way to fly home.

A turtle can swim a long way
home using its homing sense.

Super Bodies

Some animals have bodies that **sense** light.

A sea star moves around by following light.

This fish's body can sense color as well as light.

It can change its color to match what is around it!

Super Sense Detective!

Which super **sense** belongs to which animal?

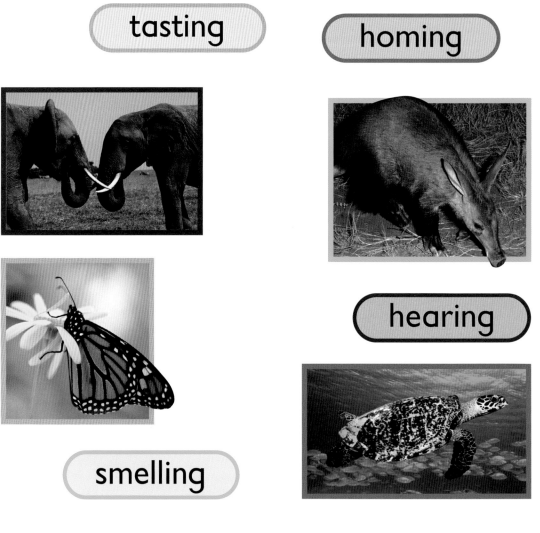

tasting

homing

hearing

smelling

Find the answers on page 24.

Glossary

 **antennae** (say *an-tan-ay*) feelers that some animals have on their heads

 **homing** a special sense that some animals have to find their way home

 sense something that helps you to see, touch, taste, smell, and hear the things around you

 **whisker** long hair that grows around the mouths of some animals

Index

Answers to Super Sense Detective:

hearing · tasting · homing · smelling

Note to Parents and Teachers

Reading for information is an important part of a child's literacy development. Learning begins with a question about something. Help children think of themselves as investigators and researchers by encouraging their questions about the world around them. Read the chapter headings. Look at the pictures. Talk about what you think the information on the pages will be about. Then read the text to find out if your predictions were correct. Think of some questions you could ask about the topic, and discuss where you might find the answers. Assist children in using the picture glossary and the index to practice new vocabulary and research skills.